AMAZING ANIMALS

Ocean Odyssey

KINGFISHER
LONDON & NEW YORK

Text copyright © Tony Mitton 2010
Illustrations copyright © Ant Parker 2010

Consultancy by David Burnie

Published in the United States by Kingfisher.
175 Fifth Ave., New York, NY 10010
Kingfisher is an imprint of Macmillan Children's Books, London.
All rights reserved.

Distributed in the U.S. by Macmillan, 175 Fifth Ave., New York, NY 10010
Distributed in Canada by H.B. Fenn and Company Ltd., 34 Nixon Road, Bolton, Ontario L7E 1W2

Library of Congress Cataloging-in-Publication data
has been applied for.

ISBN: 978-0-7534-3006-4

Kingfisher books are available for special promotions and premiums. For details contact:
Special Markets Department, Macmillan, 175 Fifth Avenue, New York, NY 10010.

For more information, please visit www.kingfisherbooks.com

Printed in China
1 3 5 7 9 8 6 4 2

To Esmé Lucia Constance McCrum
from Tony Mitton, with best fishes
For Matt and Freddy—Ant

AMAZING ANIMALS

Ocean Odyssey

Tony Mitton and Ant Parker

KINGFISHER
NEW YORK

The North Pacific Ocean
is vast and dark and deep.

It's home to many creatures
that swim and float and creep.

Here's a giant octopus.
Before you chase it, think!

It squirts whatever bothers it
with brown and cloudy ink.

Basking sharks just drift along.
That's the way they feed.

Small creatures glide into their mouths
to give them what they need.

A jellyfish swims gently.
It seems to sway and swish.

Its stinging tentacles are used
for stunning little fish.

Anglerfish are awesome.
They dangle bait that's bright.

When prey swims up to check it out,
they wait . . . and then they bite!

A giant squid looks scary.
It stares with googly eyes.

To meet a giant squid can give you
quite a big surprise!

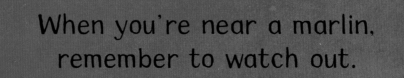

When you're near a marlin,
remember to watch out.

It's sometimes called a spearfish
because of that sharp snout.

Sea otters dive for shellfish
from kelp beds near the shore.

They tuck them in a flap of skin,
and make a little store.

Dolphins are such friendly creatures.
Meet them in the bay.

They'll come and swim beside your boat
and leap around and play.

We've drifted 'round the ocean
to find what there might be.

But were you looking carefully?
What else did you see?

Did you see . . .

the gulper eel?

the herring?

the skate?

the sea urchins?

the Dall's porpoise?

the hatchet fish?

the sea turtle?

the kelp crab?

the tuna?